# Auntie Says...
# QUICK
# WISDOM
# FOR GRADUATES

THE NIECE RELEASE

## DENEAN BENNETT

CLAY BRIDGES
PRESS

Auntie Says:
Quick Wisdom for Graduates (The Niece Release Edition)

Published by Clay Bridges in Houston, TX
www.claybridgespress.com

eISBN: 978-1-68488-039-3
ISBN: 978-1-68488-037-9 (paperback)
ISBN: 978-1-68488-038-6 (hardback)

Special Sales: Clay Bridges titles are available in wholesale quantity. Please visit www.claybridgesbulk.com to order 10 or more copies at a retail discount. Custom imprinting or excerpting can also be done to fit special needs. Contact Clay Bridges at Info@ClayBridgesPress.com.

# Auntie's Says...
## Quick Wisdom for Graduates

## Contents

| | |
|---|---|
| A Quick Heads-Up | v |
| College, Questions, and the Right Track | v |
| Let's Start with Drinking . . . | 1 |
| Now, Let's Talk about Sex | 13 |
| Let's Talk about Sex: The Mother's Note (if I were your mother) | 45 |
| Choices | 47 |
| Class and Academics | 51 |
| Own Your Time | 65 |
| The Resource of Money | 77 |
| Take Care of You | 91 |
| Security | 99 |
| Friends and Relationships | 111 |
| Social Media | 129 |
| Worship and Family | 139 |
| The Blessing | 147 |
| Acknowledgments | 151 |

## A Quick Heads-Up

Somebody probably gave you this book as a graduation gift. I bet you really wanted money, but don't be too hard on them. They want the best for you and thought what's in here could help you more than a few dollars.

Obviously, you don't have to read it if you don't want to. But you could read the whole thing in the time it takes to watch one episode of your favorite Netflix show. If you'd like to make your read even shorter, here are two suggestions:

- Read through the titles and go to the sections that interest you. If they're good, then read the rest.
- Just read the 'Auntie Says' statements. Don't get into the details unless something grabs your attention.

As any auntie would, I pray the best for you and your transition into college and adulthood. If you have questions, give me a shout: auntiesaysbooks.com, auntie_says, auntie@auntiesaysbooks.com

God bless!

## College, Questions, and the Right Track

Graduating from high school and moving on to the next chapter of your life is a very big step. Having completed that step and landing on a college campus is typically what's expected and celebrated. Whether you know it or not, while your family members are celebrating, they're also breathing a collective sigh of relief. To them, you have shown that you're planning ahead and making moves toward a life of "career progression" versus "job changes," and their concern that you won't "do something with your life" is off the table. In short, you just let them know that you've got it together.

But what if you don't?

I have a cousin that I will call Kelly. (*Her name is not Kelly. But I do not want to get in trouble for using real names, and I like the name Kelly.*) Kelly is the baby of the family. While that can be a recipe for spoiled-brat-ness, she'd outgrown much of that by the time she made it to her senior year in high school.

The summer between graduation and her freshman year in college, I spent a lot of time with Kelly. It was fun, and we grew closer. During that time, we talked about her plans for school, her career, and her life in general. I joined the group of people who said things about her like this: "She's got a good head on her shoulders." "She's so mature." "Kelly is pretty level-headed; I'm sure college is gonna go great."

Before we knew it, it was time for Kelly to start her freshman year. She headed off to campus excited and ready to tackle her college education.

The next thing you know, she was coming home for Christmas. When I asked her about school, she said everything was fine. One semester in, she had not changed her major, and she was looking forward to going back after the break.

Over Christmas break, Kelly brought home one of her best friends. Because we're cool like that, I got to spend some time with both of them. It came as no great surprise to me that Kelly's friend, who we'll call Melissa, had a "good head on her shoulders" too. She had a plan for her classes, what her career would look like, even where she wanted to live once she graduated. Melissa was on it too! I thought it was great that they would have each other to lean on for support and accountability when it got hard to stick to the plan. I was glad that neither of them was the lone, mature one in a sea of party people.

Gradually, the school information stopped coming. Kelly's sister, Vanessa, didn't have much info and always looked a little uncomfortable whenever anybody asked about Kelly. And I began to wonder what in the world was going on.

Well, it turns out that Kelly did not stick to the plan because Kelly didn't have a full plan. I came to learn that she wasn't all that good at sticking to plans in the first place. Someone who had known her while she was growing up poured me a whole cup of tea on this one: Kelly talks a good game but does not back it up with full commitment and action.

I found that hard to believe, but I couldn't deny the situation that was laid out in front of me. Kelly had failed most of her classes, mainly because she wasn't going to class. It seems she was spending a considerable amount of time with her boyfriend, and it wasn't long before we found out what they had been doing . . . and that we would have a bouncing bundle of evidence in about nine months.

Kelly made poor choices in response to temporary feelings that produced permanent results. Those results have been mostly unpleasant and very difficult for her. She dropped out of school (*it's four years later, and she hasn't returned to take even one class*); she's raising her baby alone (*she had a girl, and her boyfriend is no longer in the picture*); she's living in a roach-infested apartment with old carpet (*it's all she can afford on the money she makes working in a restaurant*), and she's not in contact with her college friends (*they're all graduating, and she's embarrassed*).

At first, this sounded like a classic case of ignored values and carelessness in the forms of sex before marriage and lack of condom usage. But when I thought more deeply, some questions came to me:

- What if things started happening and Kelly just didn't know what to do about them?
- What if she started getting Cs and, as a straight-A student, she didn't know what to do, so she shut down?
- What if she didn't know how to avoid the spiral of physical intimacy that leads to premarital sex?
- What if she didn't know how to get a handle on her thoughts and put some meat on the bones of her academic plan?

- What if the fact that she always had all the right answers covered up the fact that she felt completely clueless, that she wasn't always making good decisions, and that she just needed a little help getting on the right track?

Let's see if Auntie can cover a few things to help **you** get on the right track.

# Let's Start with Drinking . . .

*Auntie Says*

• • •

Would you leave your
dorm room unlocked
so anyone could get
in? If not, then you
should not get drunk.

• • •

*G*etting drunk is like leaving your door unlocked because it lets your guard down. Alcohol lowers inhibitions to varying degrees, depending on what and how much you eat, what and how much you drink, and your tolerance. Lowering your inhibitions to the point where you are not completely in control of your thoughts, words, and actions is NEVER a good idea.

American culture has made it seem like being completely uninhibited is the only way to enjoy yourself. Our culture has also decided that getting drunk is part of what you're *supposed* to do as a college student.

But here's what they don't tell you: If you're drunk, you are more likely to do things you'll regret and more likely to make choices that have far-reaching consequences—some of which may be greater than you even know you're signing up for. And you might not even remember most of it. Also not cool: The dollars add up and the pounds can pack on because decent alcohol is not cheap, and it's high in calories.

*About 70 percent of college students admit to having sex primarily as a result of being under the influence of alcohol.[1]*

One more thing if you don't already know: hangovers are a beast! They last much longer than the "fun" you had and are very unpleasant. You should skip them.

*Auntie Says*

• • •

Don't ever let anyone
*bring* you a drink.

• • •

hile we're at it, here's a rule that should never be broken: Do **not** ever allow anyone to bring you a drink . . . EVER! It doesn't matter who they are.

Maybe the drink they bring you has more alcohol (or a different kind) than you intended to drink.

Maybe someone has slipped something into it. (I know, that sounds like something your mom is way too nervous about, but it does happen to people.) According to a study in the *Journal of Studies on Alcohol and Drugs*, about 15 percent of female students in their first year of college are raped while drunk or drugged.[2]

*More than 1 in every 6 freshmen women are raped while incapacitated by alcohol or drugs.*

Sometimes, the drug that gets slipped in a drink wasn't even slipped in by the person who brought you the drink (especially if it's your best friend). But maybe they weren't paying attention as closely as you do, and the person who slipped it in knew you would take the drink from your best friend.

Sometimes, people are convinced that you'll like the drug but you're being a chicken and won't try it, so they make the choice for you and decide you'll think it's cool once you've tried it.

No one knows how a drug will affect your health. What if you're allergic and you die? What if they give you too much and you stop breathing? No one knows what you'll do while you're under the influence. What if you are so out of it that you have sex with the entire football team? What if you throw up all over everything for the next two hours, including the Uber? (That would cost you a $250 cleaning fee!)

Whatever . . . it's not worth it. Get your own drink.

5

*Auntie Says*

• • •

Think of unattended
drinks as toilet water.

• • •

And as you consider the first rule, here's another one: If you walk away from a drink or even turn your back on it, you're done with it . . . period!

Get another drink or don't, but don't take another sip from the one that was out of your sight. Give it to the bartender to throw out so you don't get it confused with the next one.

*Auntie Says*

• • •

I promise: You're
still an adult if you
choose *not* to drink.

• • •

You can choose not to drink alcohol. If you don't want to stand on the fact that you want to remain in control, you don't like the taste, or you just don't want to drink, then go order your drink by yourself.

Soda in a cup looks just like a drink with alcohol in it. If you just have to have the smell of alcohol to be like everybody else, order a whole cup of soda and have the bartender put a literal splash of alcohol in it.

*90 percent of all campus rapes occur when alcohol has been used by either the assailant or the victim.[3]*

One side note: Drinking alcohol is not the only way you can become intoxicated. Smoking marijuana or taking other drugs also lowers your inhibition, decreases your control, and affects your judgment. When you are intoxicated, your guard is down. When your guard is down, you may not be able to keep yourself safe.

Don't trust your safety to the people around you who may not have your best interest at heart. Take care of you.

*Auntie Says*

• • •

If you're always drinking,
you may need help.

• • •

listen, if you find that you're drunk or drinking every day, you are likely self-medicating and need help to get healthy and feel better. You may not need AA yet, but spending some time talking to a counselor is likely a very healthy choice for you.

Please do so before someone gets hurt. Your college tuition pays for both mental and physical health services; use them.

# Now, Let's Talk about Sex

*Auntie Says*

• • •

Sex changes you, and
you can't always see
the change coming.

• • •

$E$ach time you have sex, you are changed mentally and spiritually. No matter what people tell you, you cannot control or predict every outcome, especially the intangible ones.

You don't know how attached you'll become to him . . .

- Will you cry uncontrollably when y'all don't hook up anymore?
- Will you show yourself to be completely desperate by trolling him on all his social media while he's ghosting you?

You don't know whether you'll stop valuing the spiritual connection of physical intimacy . . .

- What if you inadvertently diminish the connection you could have with your future husband?

You don't know when thoughts of him and your encounters will come back to you . . .

- What do you do when they come back while you're with your husband ten years later?
- What happens when he starts popping up in your dreams while you're involved with someone else?

You don't know what he'll leave behind . . .

- Genital warts?
- Herpes?
- Chlamydia?
- One industrious sperm that starts you on a baby journey before you even know about it?

When you think about it, there are a lot of things you don't know. I'm not comfortable with that. Are you?

*Auntie Says*

•  •  •

Don't paint a target
on your vagina.

•  •  •

on't let everyone know you're a virgin. It paints a target on your vagina and sets you up as a trophy to be won.

It's not that you're not a prize. You *are* a prize because you have great value, and you have great potential. But you don't want guys only focused on you because you represent a vaginal victory to them.

*Auntie Says*

• • •

Your sexual situation
is no one's business.

• • •

*I*f someone asks you if you're a virgin, feel free to tell them it's not their business . . . because it's not.

If you think that tells the story one way or the other, you can always respond with something like, "Mind your business' or "Virgin or not, I'm not doin' it with you." Anybody who's even somewhat intelligent will understand and respect something like, "I'm staying away from being physical right now—it complicates things."

Whatever you say, thinking about it ahead of time will keep you from being caught off guard and help you own your position powerfully instead of being ashamed of it.

It's your body, your decision, and your business.

*Auntie Says*

• • •

You are worthy of
the daylight.

• • •

*I*f he can't spend time with you in the daylight—in front of people both of you know, with all your clothes on, doing things you like as well as things he likes—he *does not* deserve the privilege of your company.

*Auntie Says*

• • •

He might be a wolf in
sheep's clothing.

• • •

*J*ust because he is sweet and intelligent, defends you, opens doors for you, or talks about Jesus does not mean he's not spittin' game just to get in your panties. Be aware!

When guys are doing their best to get with you, it can be hard for you to discern what's real and what's game (i.e., fluff, flattery, and foolishness that's only meant to lull you into a false sense of love, so you'll give it up).

You can also be so busy that you're not thoroughly and accurately analyzing the situation to see how real he is. You'll enjoy the attention, and you may genuinely be fooled before you know it.

Get to know him without sex (see the "Learn to Date Without Sex" section) and get some input from a few friends. Take it slow and guard your heart. If he's not a wolf and is interested in more than sex, he'll hang in there.

*Auntie Says*

• • •

Don't take the first step if
you don't want to arrive
at the final destination.

• • •

*I*f you decide before you hang out that you're not having sex, stick to that plan even if you feel yourself changing your mind. Make *all* your choices and actions line up with not having sex, including not removing clothing and not finding yourself alone with him.

You should make decisions about engaging in sexual activity when you are not being influenced by alcohol, drugs, or his sexy self smelling good and breathing on you. When you're thinking completely sober and solo, you'll think more clearly and make a decision that's more in line with who you are, who you want to be, and the future you're working toward.

*Auntie Says*

• • •

Absolutely no sex
without latex.

• • •

*D*o *not* have sex without a condom! No matter who he is, how much y'all "love" each other, how long y'all have been together, how much he doesn't like them, how much you don't like them, whether you are on birth control, or you have a stack of Plan Bs. If he doesn't commit to this *and* stick to it—without fail—he is telling you that his desires are more important to him than your desires, your standards, and your health. Walk away!

If either of you is allergic to latex, there are several other types of condoms available at the health service on your campus and Target, Walmart, grocery stores, and even gas stations. If they're all closed, go home alone . . . it's a sign.

*Auntie Says*

• • •

Have your own condoms.

• • •

*D*o *not* rely on him to provide the condom! You won't know how old it is or what condition it's in, especially if you don't see it in bright light.

If he doesn't have one, the first one breaks, or whatever weird thing happens that makes it seem like y'all need to just go ahead without one, DO NOT DO IT!

If you have your own box of structurally sound, fresh condoms, you don't have to worry about any of that.

*Auntie Says*

• • •

Listen for the pop . . .
condoms break.

• • •

listen to be sure you don't hear the condom pop. This does happen, and it immediately puts you at serious risk for STIs and pregnancy.

If you hear it, stop him immediately and get another condom. If he's not down with that plan, he's telling you that his desires are more important to him than your desires, your standards, and your health. Walk away!

Before you have sex with him, discuss what y'all will do if this happens so that no mid-sex conversation or convincing is necessary.

*At least 1 out of 5 college students abandons safe sex practices when they're drunk, even if they do protect themselves when they're sober.[4]*

By the way, this is another time when alcohol or drugs lowering your guard can cost you. How closely do you think you're listening when you're already buzzed (let alone completely drunk or high)?

I know someone who got pregnant this way; be careful.

*Auntie Says*

• • •

Give up your panties and
you give up your power.

• • •

*W*hether you believe it or not, I can assure you of this: When you give up your panties, you give up some power.

You give up the power to be sure you're not mentally and emotionally affected by the physical and spiritual connection created by sexual contact. It clouds your judgment and therefore, your power is limited. Your power to stand your ground, demand respect, or walk away at a moment's notice if necessary is diminished (if not completely erased).

You're also trusting another human being with some very weighty things. The connection you create makes you more vulnerable to his feelings about you and about your body. It leaves you open to sexually transmitted infections, the possibility of infertility, the unintended confirmation of fertility (in the form of a baby . . . hopefully just one), a distraction from your goals, the potential of a lower standard of treatment from him and others, and a deviation from your values.

That's a lot of power to lose and a lot of trust to place in someone with nothing to lose and no binding commitment to you.

*Auntie Says*

• • •

If you get pregnant now,
I promise you the sex will
not have been worth it.

• • •

*I* have heard young, inexperienced moms say that you will never be as tired or confused or lonely or afraid or sad or hopeless as when you have a child on your own. Caring for a child alone takes away all your luxuries—those you can buy and those you cannot (like sleeping as late as you want, spending all your money on whatever you want, and not having to worry about feeding anyone but yourself).

A pregnancy is not something you can just erase with no consequences. The sex will *not* have been worth it.

*Auntie Says*

• • •

If you get pregnant and
you choose to have the
baby, you have severely
limited your options.
He, on the other hand,
has all his options and
is likely to use them.

• • •

As soon as you expose yourself to the risk of pregnancy and it happens, you've given away so many of your options. If you choose to have the baby (whether to keep it or to give it up for adoption), you have even further limited your options. Meanwhile, he has *all* his options. You cannot choose to stay or go, participate or not, tell people or not, take action or do absolutely nothing—but he can.

Even if you decide to take on all the risks and abort, he has the option to show up or not, contribute money or not, be there while you hurt or not. Once it's done, he'll walk away lighter, but the weight you carry will at times be almost unbearable and will *never* go away.

If you're pregnant and need help and answers, try: www.nrlc.org
800·712·4357
www.optionline.org
866·993·0794
Or text 313131 to chat with someone.

Sure, you can find some people who will tell you that they had an absolutely wonderful abortion experience. They had no complications, didn't sacrifice the ability to have children later, and they'd do it again. But . . .

- How do you know you'll have a great abortion experience?
- What about the fact that you're killing a whole, live person (heartbeat can be found at about six weeks)?

I'm just sayin'. . . it might not be as easy as you think.

Don't risk it.

*Auntie Says*

• • •

Any pressure to have
sex automatically means
you should not do it.

• • •

*I*f you feel pressured to have sex, that's a blinking red sign, on fire, saying that you should not do it!

You'll know you're being pressured if you feel like the expectation is hovering over you, even when you're not with him. You're also being pressured if you feel like there will be any negative consequence for not going through with it—this includes stuff he won't give you or do for you, places he won't take you, or anger he may direct at you.

You should never have sex because you feel pressured.

*Auntie Says*

• • •

Hooking up can get you
hooked before you realize
it—and not in a good way.

• • •

*I*f you engage in casual sex and do so regularly, expect to be "in your feelings" about him (yes, even more than one "him") before too long. Also, do not expect him to be in his feelings about you.

First, it is not a good idea to assume people will think, act, or feel the same way you do.

Second, he's not built the way you are. Some may not like to recognize certain biological differences, but scientists maintain that women are wired to develop attachments to their sexual partners. This can cause you to assign more meaning to the sex and every other interaction and communication, or the lack of them, than he does. You may be setting yourself up for heartbreak and bitterness.

Don't do it, girl.

*Auntie Says*

• • •

Learn to date without
sex. It's cleaner and
less complicated.

• • •

*E*very series and movie you watch makes it seem like this progression is normal: notice the person, maybe learn their first name, have a drink, and have sex. The lack of seriousness is attractive. So is the enjoyment of sex without commitment or entanglement. But that's not how it's supposed to be.

This is more of what you should expect after introductions:

> First, the two of you should do some non-sexual things to see if this person can hold a thought in his head, hold your attention, and is someone you enjoy being with.

> Then, you start to learn who he really is, what he likes and doesn't, what he believes and doesn't, how he treats people, how he treats women, how he is with money and without it, what his temper is like, blah, blah, blah.

> At the same time, he's learning these kinds of things about you too.

You can't know any of that, let alone know if you want to share your body with him (and be exposed to whatever he may or may not have) if you jump into sex right after the seventh sip of the first drink he's ever bought you.

Try a little studying at the library together. Try having lunch, getting coffee, or watching a movie. See how he behaves around your friends. See how he behaves around his friends. What I'm saying is: Take some time to get to know this guy before you have sex with him.

And another thing to be aware of is this: If you just keep grabbing new guy after new guy to scratch your sexual itch, you may learn two things: (1) the itch you're trying to scratch physically is actually a heart-thing that sex will never satisfy, and (2) you may end up with an itch (like an STI) that you can never get rid of.

# Let's Talk about Sex:
## The Mother's Note (if I were your mother)

Dear, *(insert your name here)*,

I love you dearly, and I have zero intention of raising your child.

I will **not** hold onto him or her until you finish school or be your built-in Monday-through-Friday babysitter. Your life will be irreparably changed and infinitely harder. Your former boyfriend/fiancé/baby-daddy, classmates, and friends very likely will go on with their carefree lives before the baby is out of diapers, and you will hit the brick wall you chose.

It. Will. SUCK!

If you keep your goals in front of you and work 50 times harder than you would have without the baby, you will overcome. I will love you the entire time. I will love my grandchild and will work to not make him or her pay for your actions. I will provide an appropriate level of grandmotherly assistance, but I will not enable you.

Love,

*Mama*

# Choices

*Auntie Says*

• • •

Consistently choose
to be true to the best
version of yourself.

• • •

hile in college, you will likely be in another city and responsible for yourself. Your parents and family will not know every choice you make, but God will.

Make choices that will make God and you proud. Make choices that reflect the best parts of your upbringing, your value system, and your spiritual education.

If you do that, I promise you will have a happier, richer, more productive life. You won't miss out on anywhere near as much as you think you will and, more importantly, what you miss out on will not be anywhere near as great as you think it will be.

# Class and Academics

*Auntie Says*

• • •

Unless you're dying or
contagious, go to class!

• • •

*G*o to class! Unless you are sick and cannot function or are contagious, go to class!

To prepare, it helps if you read the material that wil be covered, watch the session, and re-read (*not* skim) notes from the last class before the next class. Why?

- Reviewing material, especially on the same day it was/will be covered in class, helps reinforce the information.
- If you've already introduced yourself to what the professor will cover, you can ask questions during class that can cement or expand your understanding. This keeps you from just letting information come in one ear and go out the other, leaving you clueless during the test.
- Knowing what's going on helps keep you awake.
- Being lost in class can make you say to yourself, "I'm not learning anything anyway." At that point, you block it all out and have no chance of learning anything at all— another reason you're clueless during the test.

*Auntie Says*

• • •

When you get that
first low homework,
quiz, or test grade, get
help immediately.

• • •

*D*on't ignore the signs that you're in academic trouble. Remember, grades are indicators of two things: (1) how well you're doing what's required for the class and (2) how well you've mastered the material. When your grades drop below your true potential (and most people do have the potential to get A's), immediately take steps to correct whatever is out of whack.

That correction could be:

- Make sure you check off each requirement for every assignment.
- Raise the neatness or detail level of your work.
- Visit your professor during office hours and get your questions answered. (Bonus: The professor will know that you're putting in effort and may give you a little more grace in your grades.)
- Do more practice problems.
- Go to tutoring *more* than once a week.
- Make flashcards by hand (muscle memory does help).
- Review your notes before bed the same night you take them.
- Do whatever you know works to get back on track.

*Auntie Says*

• • •

Know when the class
drop deadline is and
respect its power.

• • •

Always be aware of that last date when you can drop a class. Put it on your calendar and evaluate your chances of doing well in the class at least two weeks before that date.

But remember, if you have study partners and tutoring help available, don't jump ship if you don't have to—you may not have those supports if you take the class later. If you have to drop because you are honestly overloaded with too many intense classes, you'll have to catch it later and pray up some help.

Dropping a class is a pretty serious thing. You can't just drop every class that is difficult or inconvenient. You'll never finish school that way.

Also, you should not underestimate the potential negative impacts of dropping even one class. Investigate thoroughly before you drop a class. Some classes are only offered in certain semesters, which means you may have to go to summer school (more $) or wait an entire year to take the class again. If you drop a class that's a pre-requisite for something else you need, your whole situation is on hold until you pass that class.

It is worth shutting down a section of your social life for a semester so you can buckle down and pass a class. It's OK to make the sacrifice. It'll only suck for a little while, but that's a more mature choice than running from the challenge. Plus, if you stick it out, that class will be off your plate and off your mind.

*Auntie Says*

• • •

Use your academic
advisor. You're already
paying for the service, and
they can save your tail.

• • •

*M*eet with your advisor and take it seriously. Prepare for the meeting.

What should you talk about? I'm so glad you asked. Ask your advisor to:

- Walk you through your degree plan and advise you on any adjustments or choices you need to make.
- Find career resources that give specific examples of how/where you can use your degree and how much money you'll make doing that job.
- Help you find professionals in a few of the jobs in your field that you can shadow.
- Help you find internships and summer job connections during your first or second meeting in the Fall. (You don't want to wait until the last minute when everyone else is looking.)
- Recommend professors who can help with finding or providing internships, summer jobs, research opportunities, and work during the school year.

Do not be afraid to ask them to do some legwork to help you make sure you're aiming your efforts in the right direction . . . that's their job. If they say it's not, ask whose job it is and make an appointment to go see them.

Get your questions answered, so every year you can make the most of the opportunities you have while you're in college.

*Auntie Says*

• • •

Don't study where
you sleep.

• • •

*I*f you can help it, don't study in your room or, if you're in an apartment, in your bedroom.

You might think that leaving home opens you up to getting derailed from studying, but here's the secret no one tells you: 80 percent of the distractions are in your own space.

If you leave to study elsewhere, you only have to fight off 20 percent of the distractions.

*Auntie Says*

• • •

If your phone is not
silenced and out of sight,
you're not really studying.

• • •

Your mom was right about this one. If you don't need your phone to *do* the studying, you should not be able to hear or see it while you're trying to study.

Silence everything except the alarm you're using as a timer and put your phone inside a drawer or bag or anywhere besides in front of you. *No, just turning it upside down will not do it.*

It's exceedingly difficult to maintain complete focus while subconsciously keeping an eye and an ear out for your next notification. Then, when you receive it, your study train of thought is derailed and has to be reestablished every time. I know, you think that's only an issue for "old people," but it's not.

Just try it for a week and see.

And no, you don't have to tell me that I was right. But, if you post it on your social media, tag me. If I include your post in my story, we can all celebrate you.

Own Your Time

*Auntie Says*

• • •

Spend time like money.

Use a schedule.

• • •

aving no structure for your days, especially your no-class days, will quickly have you wishing you could turn back time. You cannot.

Creating and following a schedule will feel like too much to do. When you first start, you'll feel like it's ridiculous and you're scheduling every minute of every day. I mean, aren't the weekends made to have no schedule? Um . . . no.

When you have a lot of time and no structure, usually you get a lot of nothing done. You may not even get a lot of rest. That's not good for you. You have a lot on your plate. You want to play hard, work hard, and rest hard.

You can start with block scheduling (see the example in this section) or something more detailed, but you need some level of structure, or you'll look up and all the time will be gone. It's not a good feeling.

Remember to include things related to:

- Academics — class, studying, breaks, study groups, professors' office hours, tutoring, meetings with your advisor.
- Hygiene — you gotta take a shower and brush your teeth.
- Self-Care — workouts, a walk, a pedicure, a massage (save up for it!).
- Chores — laundry, cleaning.
- Nourishment — cooking, grocery shopping, cafeteria meals.
- Spiritual/Mental Health — worship, counseling sessions, meditation/study.
- Fashion Maintenance — clothes shopping, shoe shopping.
- Social Life — meetings and activities for organizations you join, friends, parties, romantic relationships.

*(See? You don't have time for the hangover recovery I talked about in the "Let's Start with Drinking" section.)*

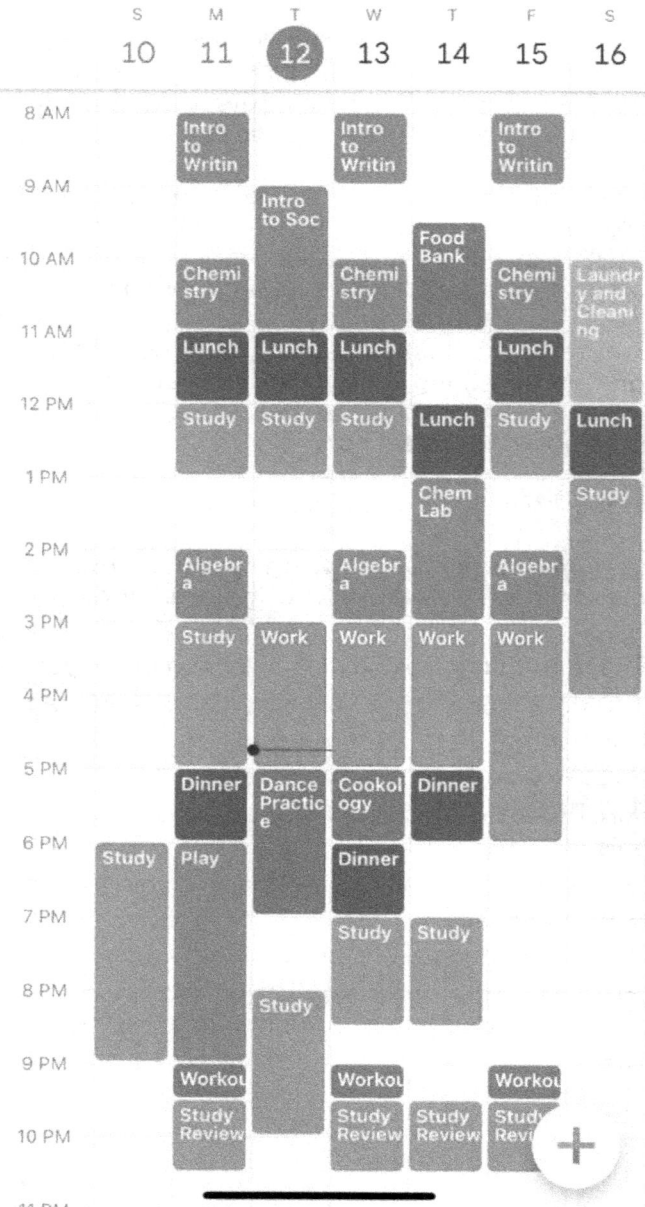

*Auntie Says*

• • •

Set goals for yourself.

You're worth it.

• • •

*D*evelop goals and do something to achieve them *every* day (at least every weekday).

At a minimum, have three short-term (0–6 months) goals, three mid-term goals (6 months to 1 year), and three long-term goals (up to 3 years). By the time you graduate, you should be able to add at least one 5-year goal.

The purpose of these goals is to create an environment that's always looking forward with expectation, not dread. You want to have something to work toward and then to have something to celebrate when you achieve it. Since your goals should reflect and inspire you, not all of them should come from external sources such as your class syllabus, work requirements, parent demands, and internship programs.

It's your life, and you should be actively in charge of where you're headed. Circumstances and new information will come that will sometimes drive you to edit a goal or two, that's OK. Adjust and keep going.

In addition to basic goals like getting at least six hours of sleep a night and making a new schedule every semester, here are a few examples of what I'm talking about:

| Target Completion | Goal |
| --- | --- |
| 0 – 6 mon | • Learn process to get internship at Johnson & Johnson<br>• Save for iPad for note-taking, sched mgmt., and life |
| 6 mon – 1 yr | • Maintain 3.5 GPA or higher<br>• Buy iPad and use it |
| 1 yr – 3 yr | • Get internship at Johnson & Johnson<br>• Pledge a service-based sorority |

One more thing to keep in mind: Your goals should be achievable but not a cakewalk. If a goal is too easy, will it even be worth celebrating when you achieve it?

*Auntie Says*

• • •

Don't let your goals
become wishes.

• • •

*W*hen Tiana (*The Princess and the Frog*) realized she was in trouble, she rolled her eyes and said: "It serves me right for wishing on stars. The only way to get what you want in this world is through hard work."

We know she learned a couple of other lessons too, but this one's definitely for you right now: Don't let your goals get watered down into wishes because you didn't work to make them happen.

Here's how to be more successful at reaching your goals:

1. Write them down. You can use notebook paper and post them on the wall, create a note on your phone, use a spiral notebook just for goals, or put them in your journal—whatever. It sounds weird, but writing goals down increases the chance you'll achieve them.
2. Whether it's daily, weekly, or a couple of times a month, consistently take steps toward each of your goals. Break your goals down and put the steps on your schedule or to-do lists and stay at it.
3. Review your goals periodically. When you start this habit, review them frequently. (I knew a guy who looked at his list of goals several times a day his entire freshman year.) You may, however, eventually settle into weekly or monthly reviews.

   This is an easy step to let slide but, at an absolute minimum, you should review your goals once per semester. The day before Finals Week every semester could work. If you tie the review to a regular date, day of the week, or event, you're less likely to forget.

   BTW, the review is not meant to make you feel bad if you haven't reached a goal. It's meant to keep you on track so the pursuit of your goals will be a regular part of your decision-making process.

   How can you expect to make choices and take actions that help you accomplish your goals if you don't keep them in focus?

*Auntie Says*

• • •

Take pics of tutoring
and office hours for
quick reference.

• • •

Snap pics or take screenshots of your class tutoring times and your professors' office hours, then save them in one album on your phone. If you're having trouble in a class, have questions, or just want your professors to see you as "more committed," you'll be more likely to show up and take advantage of these opportunities if you don't have to hunt for the information.

You should also consider taking pics of the full syllabus for each class (even if they're online). If you need to check something out, you'll be more likely to do it if you don't have to spend time looking for the syllabus.

# The Resource of Money

*Auntie Says*

• • •

Credit cards are the
devil! Well, not really, but
avoid them for now.

• • •

ay no to **all** credit cards, at least until sophomore year. The free t-shirt will not be worth the debt you will probably accumulate, the bad habits you will probably develop, and the damage you will likely do to your credit (all of which can follow you for years to come and keep you from living your best life).

Do not believe the credit card reps when they say that you need to start developing a credit history by getting your first credit card now. They don't actually care about you, beyond the fact that you will add to the number of accounts they sign up for that day.

There is some truth to the fact that there will be times when it is advantageous to have a credit history. However, it needs to be a *good* credit history.

You may not yet have the skills, the resources, or the self-control to build and maintain responsible spending habits. Without those disciplines, you are likely to become a person with bad credit. People with bad credit pay more for almost everything (e.g., higher interest rates on loans, larger deposits for utilities and apartments, higher interest rates on credit cards and car purchases). They also have a harder time getting things that they need (e.g., apartment leases, some jobs, auto loans).

No one wants bad credit, but to avoid it, you have to be intentional about how you acquire and use credit.

It may take some time to build healthy practices around spending money and planning to use money so you can develop good credit. That doesn't often happen during your first year in school. You're focused on adjusting to the freedom, responsibility, social scene, academic work, time management requirements, blah, blah, blah of your freshman year.

Use this year to train yourself to use your money wisely, and then we can talk about credit cards.

*Auntie Says*

• • •

Make your money behave:
use a spending plan.

• • •

*U*se a spending plan and track your spending. At first, it will suck if you feel restricted by the limits, but it will get easier and save you in the long run. If you don't limit and track your spending, you will overspend.

There are dozens of simple free or paid apps that will help with this, including Mint, PocketGuard, LearnVest, PocketBudget, and YNAB. Pick one and get it going. If you don't like it, pick another one.

*A year from now, you will wish you had started today.*

Just get started building this good habit. You'll be glad you did.

*Auntie Says*

• • •

Don't leave money
on the table.

• • •

ou may never again have the intersection of so much available money and so few requirements on its use; take advantage of that.

Two things:

1. Apply for scholarships like it's your job!
2. Do not believe the unspoken lie that scholarship application time is over when you graduate from high school. There are plenty of scholarships you can earn directly from your school and outside sources even after your freshman year begins and beyond.

Any money left over after tuition and fees are paid can be used for books and other expenses. You want that pile of money to be as big as possible, so get on it!

*Auntie Says*

• • •

Loan refunds are not free
money. Use them wisely
and save some because
college isn't forever.

• • •

*I*f you get a loan refund (bless you!), take 10 to 50 percent of it and do one of two things: Put it into a savings vehicle (preferably one that is interest-bearing) or invest it in an index fund that follows the S&P 500. Then, forget that this money exists until at least five years after you graduate.

If you do this every year, you may have enough to pay off any school loans in 10 years or less after graduation, depending.

*You can make a dollar out of fifteen cents if you save and invest.*

You can also use the stacks that grow from your investment to help with a down payment on your first home, your first investment property, or the start of your first business.

Don't go for short-term satisfaction on this one. Money is supposed to be a little tight in college; it's part of the experience. Do yourself a favor, play the long game and make those extra dollars work for you after you graduate.

*Auntie Says*

• • •

Don't spend it all!

• • •

$S$pend less than you make, have, or receive. When you spend every last dime, that's called "living at the end of your means." The worst part about living that way is when something that doesn't always happen happens, you're immediately relying on borrowing to keep up. And if you don't have the extra money to handle the unexpected, how will you have the extra money to pay back what you borrow (or charge on the credit card I told you not to get)? And what's gonna happen when the next unexpected thing happens? This is one way to guarantee you'll build a truckload of debt that follows you for years.

After many financial bumps and bruises, several of which occurred during my college years, I learned the 10/10/80 rule: 10 percent to the Lord, church, or help others; 10 percent to save; 80 percent to live on.

Now that I'm more exposed, educated, and experienced, I know that if you could live on 10 percent and give, save, and invest the rest, that would be awesome! That's not usually possible, so try one of the models in the table below. The larger you can make the Save and Invest buckets, the more financially prepared and comfortable, you'll be in your future.

| Financial Models to Prepare for your Future | Lord/ Help others | Save | Invest | Living Expenses* |
|---|---|---|---|---|
| Aggressive | 10% | 30% | 30% | 40% |
| Moderate | 10% | 20% | 10% | 60% |
| Conservative | 10% | 10% | 5% | 75% |

*Living Expenses are things like tuition, books, rent, utilities, groceries, fuel/transportation, cell service, clothing, and fun money. Fun money includes nails, hair, streaming services, and anything else you want but don't actually *need* to live and further your college education or work life.

If you consistently save and invest, you will be astonished at how much money you'll have five or ten years after graduation, mostly due to exercising discipline to leave the money alone.

*Auntie Says*

• • •

Don't spend your
money on stupid stuff.

• • •

Stop buying so much stuff! You know you don't need all that stuff. You don't need the newest version of everything all the time. And every year that you're on campus, you have to pack it, move it, pay to store it . . . you're just throwing your coins away.

Check yourself: If you need to have something new every week, are always buying the newest phone or carrying some expensive bag, you could be deriving your self-esteem from the wrong things. You might want to talk to a counselor about that and work on exercising some self-control.

Take Care of You

*Auntie Says*

• • •

Self-care is physical
and mental.

• • •

Your health is on a short list of things that cannot be purchased or replaced. It's also on a short list of things that directly impact everything else. Take care of you.

Don't hesitate to take advantage of health care for both your physical and mental health.

If you notice any change in your body that doesn't look or feel right and doesn't at least begin to get better in about a week, see a doctor at the student health service (which your tuition pays for). While you're waiting, list your symptoms in a note or an app, including a guess at when you started having them; they're gonna ask you.

Do not downplay or ignore your mental health because you feel weird about asking for help. When you have flu symptoms, you're not ashamed to go to the doctor for help; you make it a priority, and you get it done. Respond the same way about your mental health. If you're feeling overwhelmed *all* the time or are sad *all* the time, if you can't stop shopping or drinking, or if you can't stay focused while you're making a real effort to study, don't be ashamed to ask a counselor for help. Make it a priority and get it done.

*Auntie Says*

•  •  •

Work on your upper
body strength.

•  •  •

Females typically have weak upper body muscles. Now that you know that you should start working on improving your upper body strength. Start with curls and pushups every Monday, Wednesday, and Friday. You can start with as few as two each day and work your way up by one each week until you make it to 20 or 30 reps.

You may have to use that strength when other strong arms aren't around, and sometimes when they are. Be ready.

*Auntie Says*

• • •

Invest time in your
body and move it.

• • •

*E*xercise is more important than you might think for the proper operation of all the systems in your body. It's also quite helpful for your mental health.

Sometimes, a 15-minute walk can help you restore some order to your brain even as you strengthen your cardiovascular system.

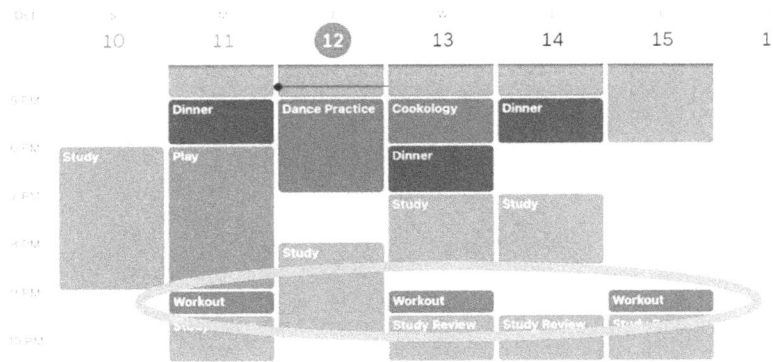

A few more things to consider:

Hydrate, hydrate, hydrate—before and after workouts and all through the day. You should drink more water than any other beverage.

*If you suspect you have an eating disorder, call 800·931·2237.*

Resist the temptation to work out in the pursuit of what may be an unrealistic body image. Remember, social media is a highlight reel of altered reality and is not real life.

Your objectives should be to feel healthy and to look healthy. If you're obsessing over every calorie you ingest and your workout results, you may have an issue. Don't hesitate to talk to a professional about it.

Security

*Auntie Says*

• • •

Guard your stuff.

• • •

Don't let everyone know about all the stuff you have or where you keep your money. Some people will use that information to steal from you. Sometimes, those are the people you think are your friends, so you're not on guard with them and share too much information. The safest thing is to not tell anybody. Why do they need to know anyway?

*Auntie Says*

• • •

Guard your other "stuff."

• • •

o not end up alone with multiple guys. It doesn't always turn out badly, but it's still not a good idea.

Travel in a mixed group. Make sure other females are around if a group of y'all are just hangin' out at the guys' apartment. Don't let the frat house become your home base.

Own it if anyone tries to embarrass you by calling out the fact that you won't be caught alone in a room or house full of guys.

Nope . . . you won't.

*Auntie Says*

• • •

Be ready for the

surprise attack.

• • •

Consider taking a self-defense class. Then, take one.

If that doesn't work for you, how about kickboxing? Those power moves have multiple uses.

*Auntie Says*

• • •

Sometimes, you just need
to be home and be safe.

• • •

hen you're tired or sleepy or not feeling well, go home and go to bed. Do not just sleep wherever you are, not knowing who may be in the room with you.

If you can't drive yourself or catch a bus, make sure your Uber fund is always ready.

You'll be safer and more comfortable in your own space.

*Auntie Says*

• • •

If it doesn't feel right,
it probably isn't.
Stop worrying about
being polite and get
somewhere safe.

• • •

You know when you're watching a movie and the girl knows that something is off, but she keeps going anyway? Next thing you know, you're yelling at the screen: "Leave girl! Just get out!!"

Well, you may find yourself in a situation where a person just makes you uncomfortable or there's something about what's happening around you that's just not right. When that happens, get yourself out of that situation immediately.

Don't worry about being polite or hurting someone's feelings by leaving; just go.

# Friends and Relationships

*Auntie Says*

• • •

Be friendly, but know
that not everyone
is your friend.

• • •

et go of your obsession with collecting as many likes, comments, and followers as humanly possible. Those people are not your real friends anyway.

Truly, if you make it to 21 with one or two real friends, you're doing great. Everyone else is basically on a continuum from "someone you kinda know" to "someone you would lend something kind of valuable to because you expect to get it back."

This is significant because you handle communication, privileges, sacrifice, sharing, and support very differently based on your relationship with each person. As an example, you wouldn't show as much vulnerability with someone you kinda know as you would with a real friend. Not everyone can be trusted with your heart and the things that are important to you.

*Auntie Says*

• • •

Know who your
real friends are.

• • •

*H*ow do you know who your real friends are?

Real friends:

- are the people you can count on to help when you need something and they don't get anything in return.
- only want the best for you, even if you outshine them.
- will celebrate with you and celebrate you, but they'll also struggle with you and sacrifice for you.
- will listen without condemning or talking down to you.
- will let you know when you're wrong as well as when you're right.
- build you up instead of tearing you down or embarrassing you.
- don't make you do all the work or spend all the money for y'all to have a good time together.
- are not constantly borrowing your stuff without returning it, while never having something you can borrow (th s is especially true with money).
- will not sit by and watch you fail without giving you a heads-up or trying to help you work through your problem (this applies to academics, relationships, finances, and other areas of life).
- will check you when what you're doing is bad for you, even if it's the new man in your life (and if they can build a solid case as to why he's bad for you, you should listen).

Make sure you know the difference between your real friends and everyone else. You want your actions and expectations to line up accordingly, so you're not left hangin'.

*Auntie Says*

• • •

If you choose to, share
boyfriend big things.
Keep boyfriend small
things to yourself.

• • •

on't tell all your "friends" every detail of how great your boyfriend (or the guy you like) is. Some people will use that information to steal from you. (See the first topic in the "Security" section.)

Understandably, you'll be excited to talk about how great your boyfriend is. And you'll like the attention you get from your friends when you tell them about how he came by and brought you ice cream while you were studying just because he knew you were struggling with biology and he wanted to make you smile. But the whole time, your "friend" Kaitlyn (or whatever her name is) is thinking about how no one ever brings her ice cream, and her boyfriend is a loser, and she low-key thinks your boyfriend is cute, and y'all aren't really that close, so it's cool if she hangs out with him and . . . and . . . well, I think you get it.

Be selective and sparing with the details and to whom you choose to give them.

*Auntie Says*

• • •

If you're always thinking
of all the ways to fix
him, move on.

• • •

No shade, but when a guy is trying to create a connection with you, he's usually putting on a bit of a show. I'm not saying that he's trying to deceive you, but he's definitely motivated to go the extra mile and put his best foot forward.

Do you know what that means? In a general sense, he may not be showing you who he is on a fundamental level, and he's likely giving you the best that he's got right now.

I'm not saying that he can't grow or choose to change. He can. But what you do not want to do is: (1) take him on as a project (like an old house to be renovated) or (2) expect that he will do anything other than stay the same or get worse. That way, if nothing changes, you're all good.

Do an honest assessment. If you're not happy with how he is right now and he's not showing any improvement, you probably need to end things as soon, and as peacefully, as possible.

*Auntie Says*

• • •

If he puts his hands
on you, walk away!

• • •

**D**o not stay in a relationship one second after he hits you. You cannot push him to any level of anger that excuses his physically assaulting you.

He should not hit you, push you, slam you against a wall, throw things at you—nothing that can or does cause you physical harm. Do. Not. Stay.

*If you're experiencing violence, go to www.thehotline.org or call 800-799-7233.*

If he apologizes 50 times by the time you make it to the door, **do not stay**. You can accept his apology and let God help you forgive him, but **do not stay** in a relationship where he can have access to do you harm.

*Auntie Says*

. . .

If he is destructive when
he's angry, you need
space and he needs help.

. . .

While there is no guarantee that he will progress from punching walls and throwing things to hitting you, I would suggest you remove yourself from the situation.

I would also suggest you consider removing yourself from the relationship entirely if he's not willing to walk into someone's office to regularly receive counseling immediately (not at some promised future time).

He likely needs help processing his emotions and identifying other ways to express his anger, but you're not his therapist, and you need to be concerned for your safety. If he cares for you and respects your opinion, he'll at least listen to what you have to say.

If he's not willing to get help, let him know that you can't stay in a situation in which you don't feel safe; then, part peacefully and immediately.

*Auntie Says*

. . .

When you're angry
enough to hit him, don't.

. . .

Guys aren't the only ones who get angry enough to throw things and take a swing at someone they care about. But being in a relationship doesn't give either of you the right to hit the other.

When an argument turns violent, someone might say, "He could have walked away." This is true. What's also true? Before the first hand was laid, she could have walked away.

Sometimes, all you both need is an hour to cool off before one of you crosses a line that you can't come back from.

*If you're experiencing rage or severe anger, go to www.safehorizon.org or call 800·621·4673.*

Do not become the aggressor that contributes to changing your relationship into an environment of violence.

Quick Reality Check: Think back to the last three times you were really angry. If your anger was on the brink of becoming violent, do something about it before it gets away from you. Seek counseling or anger management classes as diligently as you would want him to.

*Auntie Says*

• • •

Recognize verbal abuse
and walk away.

• • •

We are all guilty of responding in anger and aggravation—not giving one another enough grace. But when someone consistently degrades you, calls you names, criticizes your appearance, diminishes your intellect, makes fun of you (i.e., not being funny, but hurtful), and just all around talks back to or about you, you need to evict that person from your life.

You are worthy of being treated with respect and being celebrated for the things you bring to the table. If that's not happening, end the relationship, or at least peacefully downgrade that person to an acquaintance (no privileges).

You will likely feel like lashing out, slashing tires, and telling everyone what a horrible person you think that person is. But it's not fair to reduce someone to the worst thing they've ever done, and you don't want to be that kind of person anyway.

Choose you—move on from the friendship or relationship and connect with people who will treat you right.

# Social Media

*Auntie Says*

. . .

Don't post your tail.

. . .

o not post naked or barely covered pics of yourself. Do not post curse-filled or mean comments or rants.

I know that this type of content may seem normal to you because so many people do it across every social media platform you use. But those posts never completely go away. And, sooner or later, you will regret them.

*Auntie Says*

• • •

Your social media can
cost you money.
Be careful how you use it.

• • •

According to a recent CareerBuilder study, an average of 70 percent of employers use social media to screen candidates before offering them a position. Over half of them did not pursue hiring a candidate because of what they found in their social media accounts.[5] Even the admissions staff for some schools and programs will screen your social media and may choose to deny you acceptance because of it.

You may feel like your social media is none of their business. You may feel like there's a difference between who you are at work or school and who you are out with your friends. That's not how the world works.

Three things to remember:

1. What you put out there is fair game for everyone.
2. What you do with your friends is an indication of who you are and how you'll behave at work or campus (e.g., potential shenanigans, good or poor decision-making skills).
3. The internet is forever!

*Auntie Says*

•  •  •

Nothing digital is
ever really deleted.

•  •  •

Do not think that anything digital is permanently deleted when you delete it. It is not.

Besides that, once posts are released, anyone can capture your content, do whatever they want with it, and you have absolutely no control.

Remember that and be careful about what you post, as well as what you're doing and saying while people can record you.

*Auntie Says*

• • •

Classes have time
limits; your use of social
media should too.

• • •

It may sound like overkill, but you should plan and limit the time you hang out on social media. The occasional check, which can sometimes be a bit of a time suck, is one thing, but pouring your focus into social media platforms should be limited.

You know how easy it is to lose two hours swiping up or eft. Now that you're in school, you don't have those two-hour chunks to lose.

Put time in your schedule or set an alarm when you decide to take a break and be social. You'll keep yourself from finding out the hard way that Auntie was right about this one.

# Worship and Family

*Auntie Says*

• • •

Don't let your freedom
hold you back.

• • •

You will likely become very aware that you have the option to not go to church every Sunday. As you exercise this independence, it can become very easy to skip church Sunday after Sunday.

On Sundays, you may be catching up on rest, studying, doing laundry, and a million other things. While you do that, you limit your opportunity to feel God's love in the fellowship of believers, to continue learning and strengthening your faith, and to have people in your life who can provide additional accountability to the truths your best self has chosen to hold as your convictions.

I caution you to maintain a minimum standard of church attendance.

You may decide, for instance, that you will attend on the first and second Sunday every month, or that you'll go every Sunday except the fifth Sunday, until the desire to skip starts to die down.

*Auntie Says*

• • •

You're probably going
to miss your family.
Do something about it.

• • •

You may not believe it or expect it, but when you go away to college, you will likely miss your family. That's perfectly normal. This is especially true during your freshman year. Don't act like it's not happening, just call them or do video chats.

Understandably, you might not want to call home fee ing sad and pitiful. Who wants to dissolve into a tearful mess in under five minutes? But when you're homesick, few things will make you feel better than reaching out to your family.

It can help to have something that you share with a member(s) of your family that you can use to have what I call a "distracted connection." In other words, this will allow you to spend time connecting with them without focusing on the wave of "missing them" you're feeling.

Some of the best distracted connection opportunities can come in discussing episodes of shows you both watch, talking about the food you're forced to choose from in the cafeteria, talking about your experiences with your roommates, talking about funny stuff you found on social media, and having them catch you up on what's happening with your siblings or the neighbors.

It can also be helpful to know when your next opportunity to see them will be. Will they be coming to campus for Family Weekend? Will you be going home for a weekend soon after the semester starts, or will your first trip home be at Thanksgiving or Christmas?

When you do get to be in the same space with your people, don't spend all your time with your friends or on your phone. You will be tempted to do that. But if you do, you'll find yourself back on campus and missing them very quickly. Take the opportunity to spend some quality time enjoying them while you're together. Take pictures to use as your lock screen or display on your desktop or the walls of your room. And hang in there; your homesickness will lessen as you close in on your sophomore year.

*Auntie Says*

• • •

Even if you're not
homesick, don't forget
about family.

• • •

*I*t can be hard to stay in touch at the level your parents and family expect, but don't fall completely off the face of the earth.

Even if you have to put them on a rotating schedule in your calendar, reach out to your closest people at least once a week or so. You can use text messages, emails, and quick calls right before you walk into a class (minimum 10 minutes before the class starts; that way, you have a good reason to end the call quickly).

Yes, you're busy at school and don't want to feel like their "baby" anymore, but you do still love them. And you will definitely still want someone to send you money, buy you nice Christmas presents, and share the passwords to all the streaming services.

# The Blessing

$I$ think that's enough for now. There are probably 50 other things I could've talked about, but I wanted to focus on information that would be most useful to you.

If I didn't cover something that's an issue for you and you can't apply what's in here to your concern, please take a deep breath and reach out to the most mature person you trust or give me a shout (auntie@auntiesaysbooks.com, auntie_says).

I pray that the things I have shared in this little book will be helpful. And I pray that you will not just survive your time in college, but that you will thrive both academically and personally.

God bless!

Love,

Auntie

## Acknowledgments

My first and deepest gratitude goes to God. I thank Him for loving me, saving me, and allowing me to be a vessel for Him.

I'm extremely grateful to my husband for always being incredibly supportive of my endeavors. You have my unending devotion and thanks MD. Love, DRHDW.

Big thanks to my author mentor. Were it not for your persistence and your commitment to speak the word God gave you, who knows how long it would have taken me to publish a book.

Big thanks also go to:

- My brother, who provided support in the only way he knows how: good-natured harassment, uncontrolled chuckles, and prayer.
- My writing support team for cheering me on, reacing my manuscript, re-reading my manuscript, and sharing edits and insights. Y'all have no idea how invaluable you really are.
- My sister, who was unflinchingly positive and did not hesitate to roll up her sleeves and work to make me successful.
- My children for what they inspired on many of these pages, though they won't be able to figure out where, and for leaving me alone to write (sometimes).

I'm also very grateful to my mother for always encouraging me to not be so hard on myself, to celebrate my successes, and to write. And to my father for giving me a lifetime of witticism and, as of late, way too many bad Dad jokes. Your support and your humor are priceless.

Thank you to the people who helped me learn the lessons I'm passing on in this book. Though the experiences were not all fun, without them, I would not be who I am and could not help those who come after me.

And thank you to you. By purchasing this book for yourself or someone else, you have stepped out in faith with me, believing that God will use these words to make a difference in someone's life. I pray that He honors our intention and that He blesses every "niece" who reads it.

## Citations

1. Emma Brown, Steve Hendrix, and Susan Svrluga, "Drinking Is Central to College Culture—and to Sexual Assault," *The Washington Post,* June 14, 2015.
2. Kate Carey, Sarah Durney, Robyn Shepardson, and Michael Carey, "Precollege Predictors of Incapacitated Rape Among Female Students in Their First Year of College," *Journal of Studies on Alcohol and Drugs* 76, ro. 6 (November 2015): 829–37, doi: 10.15288/jsad.2015.76.829.
3. https://studenthealth.ucsd.edu/resources/health-topics/alcohol-drugs/statistics.html.
4. Alcohol Facts and Tips (ucsc.edu).
5. Lauren Salm, "70% of employers are snooping candidates' social media profiles," June 15, 2017, https://www.careerbuilder.com/advice/social-media-survey-2017.

CPSIA information can be obtained
at www.ICGtesting.com
Printed in the USA
LVHW080759260822
726792LV00012B/362